I'm Reading About LOUISIANA

The Pelican State!

GALLOPADE

by Carole Marsh

Printed and Manufactured in Peachtree City, GA., USA
www.gallopade.com

Book design: John Hanson

Editorial manager: Janice Baker

Louisiana is a great state.

It is one of a kind.

What makes Louisiana special?

Let's read about it

and see!

NATIVE AMERICANS

Who lived in Louisiana first?

Native Americans did!

They moved around to find food.
They hunted in Louisiana's woods.
They fished in Louisiana's rivers.
They gathered fruits and seeds and nuts.

EXPLORERS

The first explorers came to Louisiana in 1541.
They came from the country of Spain.

Hernando de Soto was their leader.
He and his men were looking for cities of gold!

SETTLEMENT

Explorers from France came to Louisiana.
They built a fort and trading post.
It became the first settlement in Louisiana.
Its name is Natchitoches!

Natchitoches was named
after an Indian tribe.

Natchitoches

STATEHOOD

Louisiana was the 18th state
to join the United States of America!

Isn't it great,
to be a state!
I bet Louisiana
could hardly wait!

Louisiana became a state in 1812.

Louisiana
The 18th State
Here we are!

FLAG

I am the state flag.

What color am I?
I am blue.

Look at me.
What else do you see?

I fly high over the state of Louisiana!

UNION JUSTICE CONFIDENCE

CAPITAL

Say hello to Baton Rouge,
the capital city of Louisiana!

There is an important building in Baton Rouge.
It is the State Capitol.
Louisiana laws are made there!

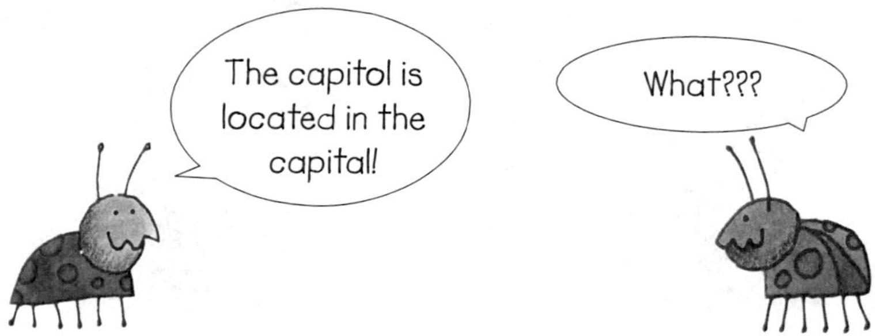

Capitol

SEAL

I am a seal,
but I am not the State Seal.
If I were, I would be very important.
I would be stamped on many official papers.
(Ouch, that might hurt!)

STATE OF LOUISIANA
UNION · JUSTICE · CONFIDENCE
Now, that's official!

NICKNAME

State nicknames are fun!
State nicknames are great!
They share fun facts
about each state!

Louisiana's nickname is "The Pelican State."

Pelicans plunge into the water to catch fish!

The Pelican State

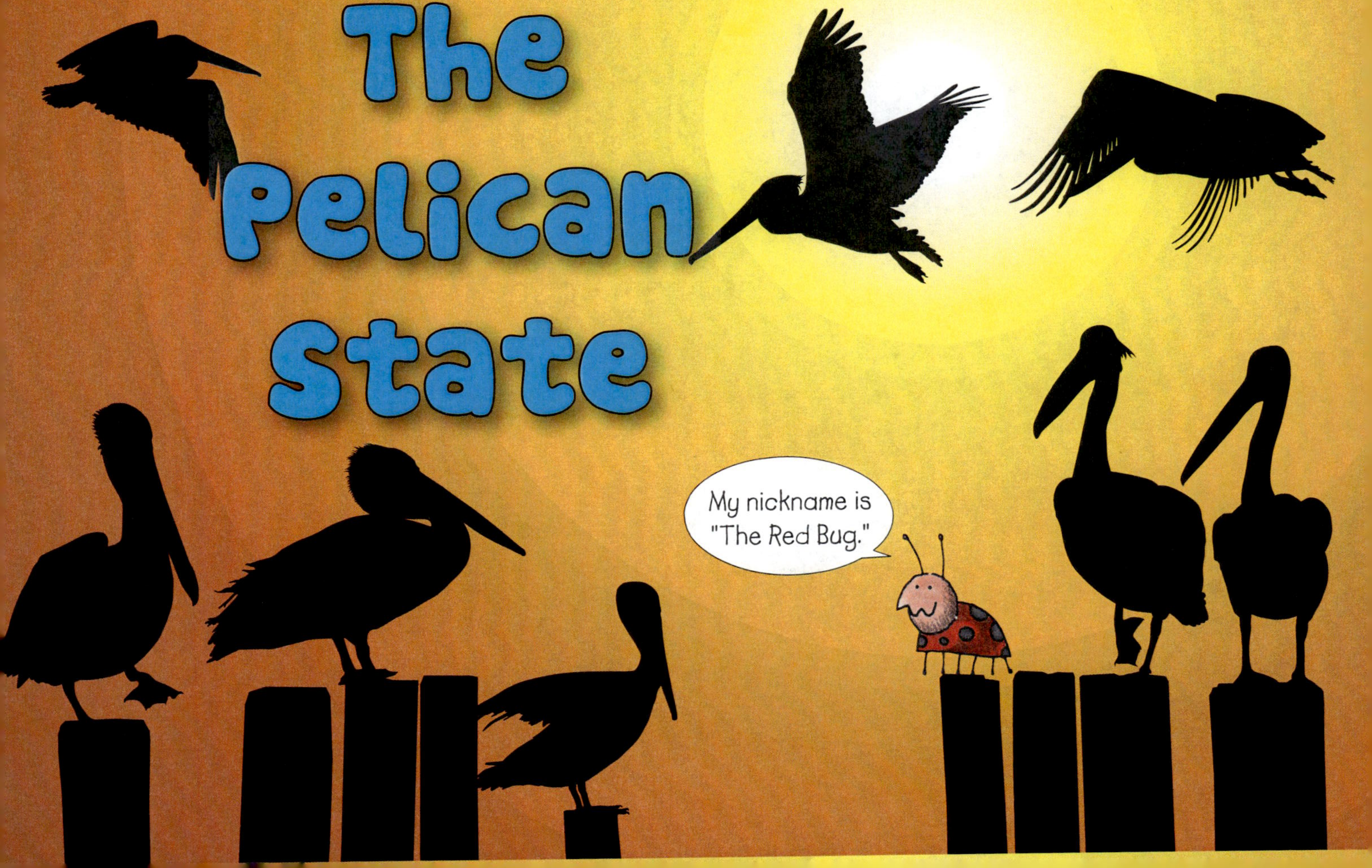

BORDERS

Look at Louisiana.
Louisiana is in a region called "the South."

Louisiana borders three other states
Find them on the map!

Borders

ARKANSAS
TEXAS
LOUISIANA
MISSISSIPPI
GULF OF MEXICO
Howdy, neighbors!

PRESIDENT

Zachary Taylor was the 12th President
of the United States of America.

Zachary Taylor grew up on a large farm.
He had seven brothers and sisters.
Zachary became a soldier in the U.S. Army.
He moved to Louisiana.
He and his family settled there.

Zachary
Taylor

Many famous people

Henry Shreve

Riverboat captain who invented a "snag boat" that cleared rivers of dead wood

Huey Long

Governor nicknamed "The Kingfish"

Louis Armstrong

World-famous jazz musician known as "Satchmo"

PEOPLE

Call our state home!

Mary Landrieu
First woman U.S. Senator from Louisiana

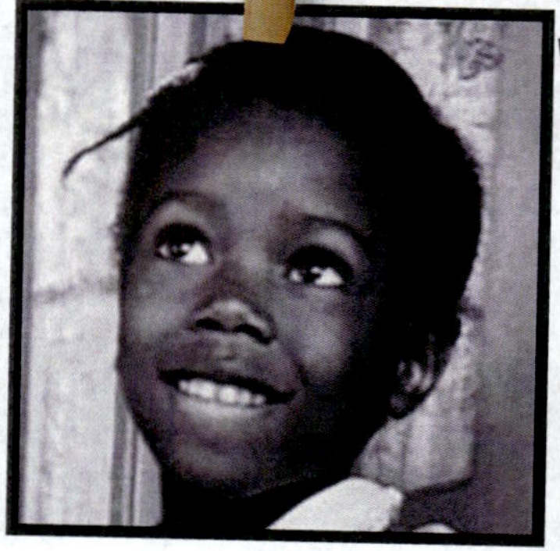

Ruby Bridges
First African American child to attend an all-white elementary school in the South

Peyton Manning
NFL quarterback named "Player of the Decade" (2000s)

Brown Pelican

BIRD

I am the state bird, and I fly
over Louisiana, proud and high.

As I fly, up in the sky,
I flap my wings to tell you "Hi!"

The Louisiana state bird is the Brown Pelican.

magnolia

FLOWER

I am the Magnolia.
I am the state flower.

I grow where it's warm and sunny.
I bloom in spring and summer.
I help make Louisiana beautiful!

Look at me! Smell me!
My leaves are thick and shiny!

Bald Cypress

TREE

I am a Bald Cypress—I'm the state tree.
Wet, swampy soil is where to find me.

My roots run deep, they keep me strong.
I can live for hundreds of years—that's very long!

I stand up straight, big and tall.
Don't climb too high—it would hurt to fall!

Honeybee

INSECT

I am the Honeybee.
I am the state insect.

I might sting you if you bother me,
But really, I am your friend.

I carry pollen from flower to flower.
I make honey.
I help Louisiana crops grow.

BZZZZZZZZZZ!

Gulf of
Mexico
Surf's up!

BEACHES

Let's go to the beach!

We can swim in the waves.
We can play in the sand.

We can build a big castle
where water meets land.

Louisiana's beaches are home to many animals:

Sea Turtles **Birds** **Crabs** **Dolphins** **and More!**

Mississippi River

RIVERS

Louisiana has many rivers.
The Mississippi River is the biggest one!

The Mississippi River is like a highway.
It runs down the middle of the United States.
It ends in Louisiana!

Atchafalaya Basin

SWAMPS

The Atchafalaya Basin is a river swamp.
It is in south Louisiana.

This habitat is home to many animals:

Birds Crawfish Snakes Frogs Alligators and More!

Do you like crawfish?
Fishermen catch lots of them in
the Atchafalaya Basin!

St. Louis Cathedral

LANDMARK

St. Louis Cathedral is a beautiful church.
It is in New Orleans.
It is one of the oldest churches in America!

The cathedral has a bell tower. The bell came from France 200 years ago. It still rings every hour!

Louisiana Crops

AGRICULTURE

Louisiana has many farms.
Why?
Because Louisiana has good soil and a warm climate!

Some of the top crops grown in Louisiana are:

Sugarcane Rice Soybeans Cotton

Sports in Louisiana

SPORTS

Baseball! Basketball! Football!
Louisiana has it all.

Whether you like to watch or play,
You are sure to have a ball!

Saints **Pelicans** **Tigers**

Ragin' Cajuns

Green Wave

& More!

Louisiana: Home of Mardi Gras

CLAIM TO FAME

Mardi Gras is a famous carnival!
It takes place in New Orleans every year.
Everyone enjoys parades, good food, and fun!

King cakes are a favorite Mardi Gras treat. Every cake has a little doll inside!

GLOSSARY

cathedral: a large, important church

climate: weather conditions in an area over a long period of time

elect: to choose someone by voting

habitat: a place where plants or animals naturally live

laws: rules made by the government

pollen: a yellow powder that helps plants make new plants

region: an area that has similar characteristics

settlement: the first community in an area

soybean: the bean of an Asian plant that contains a lot of protein

swamp: a low area of land that is often partly covered with water